ANTONY SHUGAAR

San Francisco

THE CITY BY THE BAY

Dedicated to my mother, Gerda Range, and to Elizabeth.

SMITHMARK

SAN FRANCISCO

CONTENTS

Text
Antony Shugaar

Graphic design by
Patrizia Balocco

© 1994 Edizioni White Star
Via Candido Sassone, 24
13100 Vercelli, Italy

This edition distributed
in the U.S.A. and Canada by
SMITHMARK Publishers Inc;
16 East 32nd Street,
New York, NY 10016
Tel. (212) 532-6600

SMITHMARK books are available for
bulk purchase for sales promotion and
premium use. For details write or call
the Manager of Special Sales,
SMITHMARK Publishers Inc.,
16 East 32nd Street, New York,
NY 10016; (212) 532-6600.

0-8317-7981-0

Printed in Italy by
GEP, Cremona.

1 This sign nicely summarizes some of San Francisco's most evocative places: the amazing hilly neighborhood of Chinatown, steep and festive and mysterious; the less frantic, foggier, forlorn streets of North Beach, the neighborhood of the Italians, and Union Square, the bustling, commercial, glorious center of San Francisco's businesslike downtown area.

2-3 Looking eastward, to the Berkeley Hills, this panoramic view shows San Francisco's Financial District. The two most distinctive buildings are surely the Transamerica pyramid, white and sleek and eccentric, on the left; and the Bank of America building, dark and ominous, in the center.

4-5 The Golden Gate Bridge glistens in the light of that glorious and reasonably rare event — a sunny day in San Francisco. Ships and swirling currents sweep in and out.

6-7 Lombard Street, certainly one of the most crooked streets in the world, as the San Franciscans themselves like to bill it, is also one of the floweriest, and probably among the steepest. It is also paved entirely with red bricks, which just makes for more squeaking and skidding.

8-9 During the construction of the Golden Gate Bridge, a number of problems had to be solved, chiefly because of the rushing waters of the ocean currents and the violent winds.

10-11 A view of the Yerba Buena Center, a new urban project across the street from the Moscone Convention Center; this center brings art, theater, and the café life to an area previously listless where not actually blighted.

12-13 Built in 1936, the Bay Bridge, which links San Francisco to Oakland and Berkeley, extends over the bay for four and a half miles, and extends, land-and-water, approach-to-approach, over eight miles.

INTRODUCTION

Any book about San Francisco should begin by talking about the weird, almost dreamlike aura in which the city wraps itself, perched on hills amidst wraithing mists, overlooking the turbulent waters of the bay that have been sung by poets such as the two Jacks — London and Kerouac — and by Hammett; perhaps comparable, in terms of its landscape and setting and attainment of classical literary stardom, to only one other American city: New Orleans. Yes, of course, San Francisco is much more than the fey, twee, dreamlike aureola that the city sells retail: it is a real city, with all the attendant problems that implies. Yet San Francisco maintains its amazing Taoist charm, like some piece of landscape that has escaped from an ancient

Chinese painting: though thousands of tourist roam wonderstruck through the town everyday, it remains a liveable and eminently lovable place. No amount of marketing seems able to rob the city of its magic. Take Ghirardelli Square, for example; this splendid piece of pseudo-Gothic red-brick architecture, is stuffed, like some three-dimensional Advent calendar, with souvenir shops and postcard stands. Yet, amidst the claptrap and cellophane, you will find shelves full of scented candles and granny glasses, reminders of the Summer of Love, of San Francisco's torrid youth, of an era gone by. In a city this lovely, it is impossible to resent the tourist industry: it seems only logical to bring as many people to gaze upon this incredible city of hanging gardens, streets steep as roof tops, and towering buildings. Cable cars, eternal denizens of the hills, are incapable of corniness, no matter how shameless the posing of the cable-car operators and no matter how square and un-SanFranciscan the passengers. This cog-railway amidst the clouds is pure mechanical joy, no matter how high the fare rises, and no matter how many sorry

14 Several of the moored historical ships of the Aquatic Park, among them an 1890 ferryboat named "Eureka" and a three-masted wooden schooner; an old sidewheeler, the "Eppleton Hall"; and the "Balclutha," a 301-foot three-masted Scottish merchantship that sailed around Cape Horn seventeen times.

15 This is an aerial view of Ghirardelli Square, Fisherman's Wharf overlooking the bay, and the Aquatic Park, with its moored historic ships.

16 This is the gleaming white tip of the Transamerica Pyramid Building, atop forty-eight stories of financial transactions and mysterious networks of holding companies. The building was erected in 1972, and although its odd cobra-like hood gives it a certain allure, many old-time San Franciscans still rue the block of buildings that were razed to make way for it: the only buildings to survive the 1906 earthquake.

17 A parade of allegorical choruses, a lively mural, and the inevitable cable-car, enliven the streets of San Francisco, emphasizing the joyful character and the relaxed atmosphere of this singular city.

imitations besmirch the streets. One forgives the city everything, however, when, in the early morning, climbing Russian Hill and passing the intersection of the Powell and California cable-car lines, you hear the heady whirr of the huge, powerful cables as they run through their sprockets and sheaves, gallopping along beneath the tracks and concrete with all the power of a hundred horses... San Francisco's dreamy wonder is this: the present here seems like a particularly pleasant memory. The San Francisco experience lies in the simultaneity of past and present: it is no accident that the city has chosen as its anthem a song about leaving one's heart there. After leaving San Francisco, you inevitably long to return; as Oscar Wilde once said: "Anyone who disappears is said to be in San Francisco; it must possess all the attractions of the next world." It is a city of personal experience, offering memories of every sort. The comedian Bill Cosby did a routine called "San Francisco in a Volkswagen" in which he summoned up memories of unrelieved fear. Having, myself, driven San Francisco in something slightly worse than a VW — specifically a Fiat 600 — I confirm Cosby's description of his own thoughts at finding himself in a classic San Francisco motorist's dilemma. His car was perched dangerously — nose-up, tail-down — at the crest of a colossally steep incline, brake-pedal jammed down and clutch poised on the brink of panic; Cosby had just urged his little vehicle up the hill to its utmost, gaining the crest only to be halted by a red stoplight. "Look, Martha," Cosby imagined a man saying, as the same man peers out at Cosby's VW, from behind the blinds at the first-floor corner window, holding a small push-button remote control leading to the stoplight. "I caught another one." Equally interesting is the bicycle-messenger's experience of coasting down Lombard Street, the twisty, brick-paved, flower-lined lane that pitches one-way

18-19 One of the most controversial developments in San Francisco during the Seventies and Eighties was the so-called "Manhattanization" of the Financial District. Here one can see the canyons of architecture that no San Franciscan would have recognized as part of the city just thirty years ago. Tucked away here and there, but clearly recognizable as such, are some of the earlier tall buildings of the city.

downhill at a 45 degree grade, on a Schwinn messenger bike with coaster brakes and a front basket. As a former Speedy's Bicycle Messenger in San Francisco, I can tell you: It's fun. The bike tires slide squealing across the bricks in a controlled drift, angling on the leverage of the wheels' gyroscopic force, a two-wheeled slalom as exhilarating as it is dangerous. Bill Cosby also theorized that the flowers along Lombard Street might mark the graves of so many motorists, unequal to the challenges of the alarmingly steep streets. And yet San Francisco's vertical nature makes it the most stunning of cities: almost everything is made more dramatic when one looks straight down at it, or gapes straight up at it, or surveys it from a perfect vantage point. In particular, one can almost always see the spectacular 450-square-mile bay, stretching out into the distance. As the ingenious-if-smug city chronicler Herb Caen — star columnist of the San Francisco Chronicle for decades, and inventor of the pet name "Baghdad-by-the-Bay" — puts it, "This is the only city you can lean against when you get tired of walking around in it." This same quality of steepness makes San Francisco an exhilirating city, as well as a picture postcard wonderland. No one will ever be able to forget the San Francisco evoked by Steve McQueen's stunt-car driving at breakneck speed up, down, and especially sailing over the crest of San Francisco's portentous hills, in the great action film "Bullitt." As a bicycle messenger in the city, I had some Bullitt-like experiences, fortunately at lower speed. I did once attain stunt-car speed in a flatout run down California Street toward the water. I had decided to let the bicycle rip, and after several blocks at terrifying velocity, I passed a pickup truck, and was able to glimpse the speedometer: 50 mph. A couple of blocks ahead pedestrians were crossing at a light; I leaned the bike into the controlled skid that was surely to ensue, and stepped

19 top Dolores Park lies at the intersection of Twentieth and Dolores Street, one of the prettiest boulevards in the city. Just four blocks away stands Mission San Francisco de Asìs, also known as Mission Dolores.

22-23 More than half of the Bay Bridge's length of four and a half miles spans the water of the bay; the lower span runs toward Oakland, while the traffic on the upper half is heading for San Francisco.

20 The Painted Ladies, as San Franciscans refer to the Victorian homes built here between 1850 and 1915, are distinctive in their fanciful blend of gingerbread, art deco, columns, geometric and floral shapes, and stained glass.

21 The Alamo Square Historic District lies just east of the beginning of Golden Gate Park, and not far from Buena Vista Park; this is the so-called Steiner Street "Postcard Row," popular in photographs with its Victorian foreground and downtown-skyline background.

onto the footbrakes. Rubber squealed as I skidded down two full blocks of California Street, coming to a halt just a few feet short of a crosswalk full of startled pedestrians. And if San Francisco is a roller coaster of two- and four-wheel excitement, it is also a city of lyrical poetry, a city that one cannot easily forget. You really can leave your heart in San Francisco. San Francisco is a textbook example of what constitutes a romantic setting: creeping fog, dramatic wind, sad slow drizzles, and sweeping titanic views. It is also a city with one of the loveliest public parks ever built — Golden Gate Park. Running amidst redwood and eucalyptus groves, out to the great Pacific shore, the park is dotted with art museums, Japanese gardens, boulders and fountains. During the hippie years, I once saw youngsters wandering through the Park's spectacular rose garden under a light rain, gently and sensuously kissing dew-splattered rose after dew-splattered rose. It is a city that deserves its park. And San Francisco, rightly or wrongly, seems to be a city that conceals entrancing, exotic mysteries. One of the mysteries I witnessed was anything but a mystery, in the end, and yet worth the telling. I was riding with several deliveries in my basket, heading up a long straight hill. A bearded man came walking down the hill toward me on the sidewalk, a dark smudge on his forehead. A few dozen yards further on, a grandmotherly women walked downhill, a smudge on her forehead too. As I groaned my way up the hill, more and more people appeared, foreheads smudged with ash. Who were these people? Why the dark smudges? Until I reached the Catholic church, out of whose doors streamed faithful worshippers with ash-smudged foreheads, I had forgotten that today was Ash Wednesday; San Francisco is a city of Catholic immigrants, and yet I still cannot help but wonder absently at times about the secret cult rituals I had imagined as solutions to the mystery.

PORTRAIT OF SAN FRANCISCO

It is a tall city, rising at the northernmost tip of a thumb-shaped peninsula, poised just opposite what could be an index-finger curving southward. If the San Francisco Bay represents, roughly, the 0-shape enclosed by finger and thumb, then the analogy is complete. The index finger curving southward is Marin County, home to political liberalism of California's very silliest sort, philosophers, self-help gurus, ex-hippies and ex-advertising execs living on houseboats, master stained-glass makers, potters, cabinet makers, plenty of successful professionals, and enough therapists to cure the population of Twin Peaks (the imaginary town out of director David Lynch's bad nightmare, not the section of San Francisco by the same

name), several times over. Sausalito, the closest point to San Francisco in Marin County, is a lovely quay-front town of espresso bars and expensive gift shops, bakeries and frisbee shops, twee restaurants and health-food stores. From the quay it rises steeply, and high up in Sausalito's hills are houses and restaurants with some of the finest views of San Francisco to be found. Sausalito is linked to San Francisco by proud blue and white ferry boats that ply the headwaters of the bay: running from the Ferry Building, at Pier 1 (roughly where Market Street intersects with California Street not over two hundred yards from the bay) over to the Sausalito waterfront — where Robin Williams once washed dishes in a macrobiotic restaurant. Across the San Francisco Bay, to the east, lie the cities of Berkeley and Oakland. Berkeley has a decades-long tradition of radical politics and loose-screw eccentricity, and boasts one of the finest universities in the country. High in the auburn hills above the huge campus of University of California at Berkeley stands the Claremont Hotel, a grand and palatial structure dating from other

24 Since San Francisco stands just a few miles from the San Andreas fault, the taller buildings and the skyscrapers have been built to withstand even the most intense earthquakes.

25 Columbus Avenue, which runs from Washington Street down to the Transamerica Pyramid Building, is the only street that cuts through downtown on a diagonal.

times. The interior is all that an Edwardian hotel could be; employees secretly slide down the labyrinthine laundry chutes that wind downward the entire height of the building. Berkeley — the groves of academy with a healthy scattering of populist lunatics.

To the south is Oakland, about which Gertrude Stein once said, unjustly, "There is no there there." The city of Oakland is an alternation of urban blight and Victorian charm, and Chez Panisse, one of America's finest restaurants, is there. And to the north lies Richmond, and beyond the Carquinez Straits, is Napa Valley and the wine country. To the south, along the Peninsula, lies San Jose, a metropolitan area now as large as San Francisco itself. Further south still is Stanford University and Silicon Valley, birthplace of the computer revolution.

Along the Pacific Coast, north and south of the city, are some of the most enchanting coastline drives in the world, fog-wraithed, steep, and remarkably similar to Chinese paintings of the facing Pacific coastline, thousands of miles away. And, inevitably, one makes comparisons — San Francisco is one of the world's great and beautiful port cities, ranking with Istanbul, Sydney, Rio de Janeiro, Hong Kong, Capetown, Genoa, and Naples. And, in a statement that may have revealed the greatest intuitive understanding of the city's somewhat austere beauty, Sophia Loren once said, "Your city is so very beautiful, I think more beautiful than Naples, but not so romantic." San Francisco once had a different international stature than it has today — the Japanese final surrender in World War II took place here, the League of Nations was founded here, the Zimmerman Telegram, with all its German intrigue in Mexico, was sent here — and part of the stature of San Francisco developed out of its open-minded, universalist, vaguely socialist mindset; no one exemplified that mindset more thoroughly than Dashiell Hammett.

26 A cable car, heavily laden with tourists and in the capable hands of the "gripman," runs tightly attached to a huge underground cable that pulls it effortlessly up Hyde Street, heading for the top of Russian Hill and then down Powell to Market Street.

27 top Built on the slopes of more than twenty hills, and girded on three sides by salt water, San Francisco is clearly an unusual city, whose streets are in some places steeper than thirty degrees.

27 bottom The Financial Center of San Francisco has undergone considerable upward development over the last few decades. The shorter buildings generally date from the years prior to 1965. After that date, in fact, the taller skyscrapers were built.

28 San Francisco is a remarkably green city: the public gardens, parks, and play areas are cared for very well, and so are the private gardens of the houses on the hills. This is also true of Fort Mason, a former military structure, now a recreation area inside Golden Gate Park.

29 The remarkable structure of Saint Mary's Church, just west of the downtown area, has excited a great deal of comment in this architecturally conservative city; some San Franciscans have compared its modern shape to the agitator of a washing machine.

30-31 In the area south of Market Street (colloquially referred to as SoMa), Yerba Buena Garden, an enormous piece of architecture and landscaping, is meant to restore panache and luster to a neighborhood of industrial decay, in Mission Street between Third Street and Fourth Street.

Hammett was the inventor of the hard-boiled detective, Sam Spade, who made cynical pragmatism romantic: "I'm going to send you over, darling," was his way of telling the woman he'd fallen in love with that he would be turning her over to the police for murder, in "The Maltese Falcon." And yet that hard-edged open-eyed been-there done-that realism continues to characterize San Francisco, making it a tolerant, civilized city that puts up with eccentricity bordering on the pathological.

Another adoptive San Franciscan — around the time of the Be-Ins and the first concerts of the Grateful Dead, Jefferson Airplane, Doors, Janis Joplin, and Jimi Hendrix — was Emmet Grogan, founder of the Diggers. Grogan was a bad street kid from New York who had been accepted at age 15 into an elite preparatory school on the Upper East Side in the late Fifties. Grogan kept his eyes open everytime he was invited to a Christmas party at the end of the first semester: he was in fact casing the apartments. When all his rich classmates and their families left town on their extended Christmas vacations, the penniless Grogan remained in town with nothing but a lot of floor-plans and a hunger for quick cash.

Agile as a monkey or a cat, Grogan made his way into a dozen of his classmates' apartments, and then fled to Europe with fifty thousand dollars' worth of swag. Upon his return from Europe in the mid-Sixties, the twenty-three year old Grogan could find only one place in the U.S. fantastic enough to attract him: San Francisco. He arrived just as the hippie movement was beginning to gather way, and founded a loosely organized group called the Diggers, who would beg, borrow, or steal food in industrial quantities to feed the hippies that were reaching the city in ever-increasing numbers. This too is the spirit of San Francisco: the capacity to thrive amidst uncontrolled anarchy.

32 The uniform blue of the San Francisco Bay softens the strict and severe outlines of the downtown skyscrapers.

33 In this panoramic view, the skyscrapers of downtown jut skyward, showing all their power and wealth.

SAN FRANCISCO

34 top Futuristic structures distinguish the area south of Market Street; this is the Moscone Center, symbol of a major drive for urban renewal.

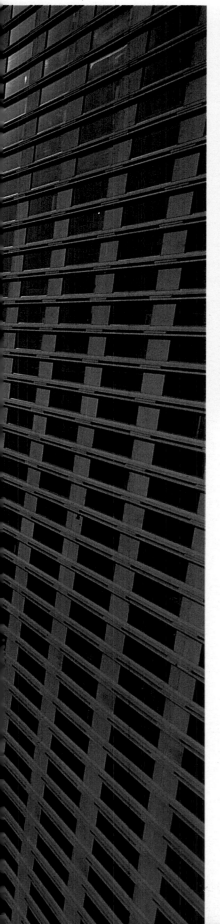

34-35 Street furnishing from the waterfront area of the Embarcadero, which has been undergoing some reconstruction ever since the destruction of the Embarcadero Freeway, badly damaged in an earthquake. This odd piece of work is perhaps more Las Vegas than it is San Francisco, in stylistic terms.

35 This photograph of the Transamerica Pyramid Building, at the terminus of Columbus Avenue in the heart of the Financial District, emphasizes its odd, pyramidal construction, and its architectural heartlessness.

36-37 A view up Market Street looking east: to the left is San Francisco's City Hall, looking very much like St. Paul's in London; in the distance is the Financial District with its skyscrapers, and the Oakland Bay Bridge.

38 In the foreground, one can clearly see the island of Alcatraz; in the background loom the skyscrapers of the Financial District. Alcatraz became a Federal penitentiary in 1934, and, because of its location, was soon designated as a prison for the most desperate and dangerous criminals, including Al Capone and the famous Machine Gun Kelly. It was shut down in 1964.

39 High winds and choppy waters are the standard fare for sailboat captains braving San Francisco Bay in even the sunniest of weather. This is the city that gave birth to Jack London, poet of the ocean waves and Alaskan snows.

SAN FRANCISCO

40 top The Columbus Tower, at the corner of Kearny Street and Columbus Avenue, is one of the city's earliest "skyscrapers."
It was already under construction when the earthquake hit in 1906. It marks the confluence of downtown, Chinatown, Jackson Square, and North Beach. It is now owned by the film maker Francis Ford Coppola. In the background is the Pyramid Building.

40-41 Over the top of Nob Hill comes the Powell Street cable-car, about to start its descent at the same phlegmatic rate of ten miles per hour at which it makes its climb. Situated behind Union Square, Nob Hill takes its name from a popular mispronunciation of "nabob," the standard fauna to build houses atop the city's choicest real estate.

41 top This awning and portal at 1201 California Street is a classic example of the Spanish Revival style that was so popular in this city during the Twenties.

41 center Nôtre Dame des Victoires, long considered to be San Francisco's "French" church, was first built in the 1850s. After the 1906 earthquake, it was entirely rebuilt as it stands today, a replica of a Catholic church in Lyon, France.

41 bottom The original structure of the Mission Dolores was built in 1781. The bell tower, shown here, abounds in ornamental decorations, and is part of the church built in 1916.

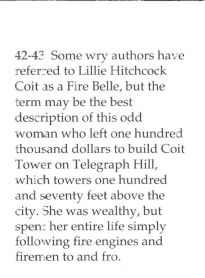

42-43 Some wry authors have referred to Lillie Hitchcock Coit as a Fire Belle, but the term may be the best description of this odd woman who left one hundred thousand dollars to build Coit Tower on Telegraph Hill, which towers one hundred and seventy feet above the city. She was wealthy, but spent her entire life simply following fire engines and firemen to and fro.

44-45 The monument that stands in the center of Union Square was built to commemorate the spectacular victory over the Spanish fleet in Manila Bay in the Philippines in 1898 during the Spanish-American War, under the command of Admiral George Dewey.

46 The fading light of day seems to linger on the tip of the Transamerica pyramid, which r_ses above the surrounding skyscrapers.

47 The gentle light of sunset is reflected on the facades of the skyscrapers, creating an attractive glow.

48 The Palace of Fine Arts was designed by the noted Berkeley architect Bernard Maybeck as a temporary construction in 1914 for the Panama-Pacific International Exposition, celebrating the opening of the Panama Canal. As Patrick McGrew, an architectural historian, puts it, "Visitors were captivated by its beauty, and efforts were immediately undertaken to have it reconstructed of permanent materials. But half a century would pass before this was accomplished."
The structure is now an art museum, with the ceremonial colonnade and rotunda. The latter structures are accurate reproductions of the originals, while the building was simplified to reduce expenses.

49 The Palace of Fine Arts, which is reminiscent of the temples of Ancient Rome, was rebuilt, thanks chiefly to the generous two-million-dollar bequest of Walter Johnson, a San Francisco businessman. Nowadays, the palace houses the Exploratorium Science Museum, and an auditorium.

50-51 The glittering structure of the Hall of Flowers, which stands inside Golden Gate Park, was built in 1878, in the purest of Victorian styles, using the exquisite Dublin crystal. The design was based upon the Palm House in London. The greenhouse contains more than five thousand varieties of plants.

52 The great expanse of Ocean Beach, once the site of a huge and tawdry amusement park. The water is far too cold for swimming; at the turn of the century the world's largest swimming tank, long since demolished, was built out here, and named the Sutro Baths. It is here, more than anywhere else, with the rollers rising taller than the line of sight, cutting off the horizon, that San Francisco seems like land's end.

53 Cliff House, as it stands today, is a fairly bland piece of architecture in an astonishing location. The original Cliff House, on the other hand, was a remarkable Gothic castle destroyed by fire the year after the 1906 earthquake. On the right stands Seal Rock, covered with seagull guano and the wriggling bodies of many California brown seals.

LIFE IN THE STREETS

I myself had a particularly intimate view of the streets of San Francisco. I was a bicycle messenger in San Francisco for a year, in the early Seventies. I was fifteen. I rode out of Pier 3 - with Speedy's Messengers — wearing a white cotton jacket embroidered Speedy's, a walkie-talkie on my belt, pedalling a yellow Schwinn Heavy-Duti, with basket, that weighed close to sixty-five pounds.

Think of it — a bicycle messenger in San Francisco. The city is all hills and flatland, a series of roller-coasters and safe landings for the budding messenger.

I arrived by bus every morning from Berkeley, where I lived, crossing the massive grey Bay Bridge, perched high in a city bus, looking down hundreds of feet onto cold

grey water. A cup of coffee, nutty creamy and sweet, in the old diner at the corner of Pier 1, and then onto our bikes for the morning's first delivery. I rode the city with all sorts of merchandise; everything from airplane tickets and stocks and bonds, to huge styrofoam cases containing live lobsters. My first, regular delivery involved a ride along the waterfront, in the shadow of the Embarcadero Freeway, long since demolished; under the piers of the Bay Bridge, where traffic thunders along on five lanes on the bridge's lower level. There is an astonishingly fine smell of roasting coffee throughout this neighborhood in the early morning air, at the top of Howard Street hill, owing to a nearby coffee factory. Down the Howard Street hill, to the flatlands; a straight run along one of the five or six avenues running parallel south of Market Street. Here, a slight geographic parenthesis should be opened: if the San Francisco peninsula is thumb-shaped, we can imagine a thumbnail at its northernmost tip. In that thumbnail, downtown San Francisco occupies the uppermost third on the right, on the bay side of the

54 The only city in the world, according to columnist and local folk-legend Herb Caen, where — once you get tired of walking around in it — you can just lean against it. These cars are parked in the safest way possible on the very steep Vallejo Street, atop Russian Hill.

55 Lombard Street, located on Russian Hill, begins at High Street and runs all the way to Heaven Worth, winding through ten steep hairpin turns.

SAN FRANCISCO

57 Union Square, with its column dedicated to a great naval victory in a fairly minor war, the Spanish-American War of 1898. This square has become one of San Francisco's most chic and expensive little shopping areas. In the foreground is Maiden Lane.

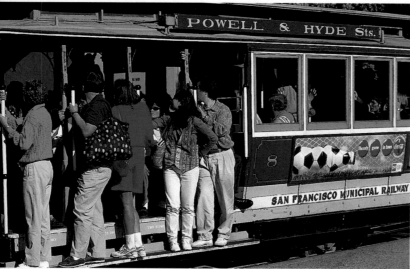

56 top Every once in a while even the most dedicated lover of everything that is San Franciscan is dealt an aesthetic body-blow; this twee fake London double-decker brings loads of tourists through the city, depositing them in the various tourist zones throughout the city, notable among them Ghirardelli Square.

56 bottom The speed of the cable-cars is the same going uphill and downhill, about ten miles an hour. These unusual means of transportation were declared a national historical landmark in 1964.

peninsula. Market Street runs southwestward from the northeastern tip, where the Bay Bridge reaches over from the East Bay. Like in some giant harp, Market Street forms an angled base; south of it, mighty flatland avenues run parallel to it; north of it is hill country, and streets angle away from Market, running one north, one west, one north, one west. Queen of the streets running west from the water's edge, California Street runs sharply uphill, rutted by two humming cable-car tracks.

Halfway across downtown, Powell Street is the central abscissa of the quadrant or grid; running north-south this is the route of the Powell-Mason cable-cars that run out to Fisherman's Wharf. At Powell and Market and at California and Market are cable-car turnarounds; at Powell is a turntable, still turned by the conductor and brakeman in their khaki bolero jackets; at California is a gauntlet, where cars change track. Further west, parallel to Powell, runs Van Ness, the boundary of downtown; the northern boundary is Fisherman's Wharf and the Embarcadero. Up and down the strings of this giant lyre, up and down the hills immortalized in "Bullitt," I rode my yellow no-speed, coaster-brake Schwinn.

Along Market — at times daring the other messengers to ride between the Market trolley cars, daring the scant three-inch clearance on either side of the handle bars; north on Van Ness — amidst the racing uphill traffic, all the way to the Marina and east to the tourist mecca of Ghirardelli Square and Fisherman's Wharf. Between Van Ness and Powell — closer to Market — is the Tenderloin, a wasteland of XXX theaters and bad neighborhoods: bad in the tradition of Errol Flynn, who once said, "I always see about six scuffles a night when I come to San Francisco," adding, "That's one of the town's charms." North of the Tenderloin, between these two streets, lies Russian Hill, one of the city's most remarkable areas.

The Sixties super-model, Twiggy, once declared, in a burst of mod expressionism, "It looks like London and Paris all stacked on top of each other." Russian Hill — along with nearby, more properly downtown Nob Hill — is where most of the stacking is done. Both cable-car lines run here; it was not of this hill, however, but of its neighbor, that Rita Hayworth was thinking when she made the following, evocative statement: "I like the way the wind whips your skirts when you go by cable-car up Nob Hill." No skirts are whipped by the wind when you go by bicycle up Nob Hill, or Russian Hill, this ex-messenger can assure you. And it is only by bicycle that one can appreciate the extreme steepness of the streets, the exhilaration of conquest upon reaching the peak. Atop Nob Hill are several extremely posh hotels. Atop Russian Hill are many three-, four-, and five-story buildings, but only two genuine towers: apartment buildings rising to twelve or fifteen stories, with amazing views of the bay. Wraithed in mist, these buildings tower above the silence of wind and fog; from the street, they seem framed in the neat interstices of tram and electric-bus cables; at their foot, but atop the hill, is a wild little park. From here, one can see both Golden Gate and Bay Bridges. Further downhill, is Coit Hill, topped by Coit Tower, erected by a wealthy San Francisco matron in memory of her husband, a fireman. The tower, in fact, resembles the shape of a brass fire hose. And, down on the waters of the bay itself, every so often one can spot the harbor-dredging ship, to all appearances a tramp steamer, with a castle set in a red circle on its smoke stack, white stanchions along the sides, and green trim, straight out of a story by Joseph Conrad.

58 Among the many department stores overlooking Union Square, Neiman Marcus is certainly one of the most elegant and exclusive; it is topped by a distinctive art deco glass cupola.

59 top This is the remarkable interior of Nordstrom's department store on Market Street, a canny borrowing of architectural motifs ranging from the Guggenheim Museum in New York, the Galleria in Milan, and Le Printemps department store in Paris.

59 bottom This photograph shows the main entrance of the Neiman Marcus department store, where one can also dine on refined international cuisine.

SAN FRANCISCO

60 top left The Fairmont Hotel stands at the intersection of California Street and Mason, high atop Nob Hill. It was originally the site of the home of James Fair, who was a Comstock silver king, as was William Randolph Hearst; clearly Nob Hill supplied the "-mont" ending, and the Reid Brothers supplied the architecture of the hotel that replaced Fair's home in 1902-6.

60 top right Seagulls sport and frolic in the clear waters of this lovely little fountain in the Yerba Buena Gardens, a brand new project just south of Market Street; the complex features an art museum and performing arts theater.

60-61 One of the nerve centers of downtown San Francisco is the Powell Street cable-car turn around, at the intersection with Market Street. Here the cars are still rotated on an old-fashioned turntable, a curiosity that attracts many tourists.

61 In this picture, one can see the remarkable terraced architecture of San Francisco's Hyatt Regency Hotel at the foot of California Street.

62-63 The Powell and Market Streets cable-car runs up from Fisherman's Wharf, loaded with tourists and locals. It is possible to only take a glimpse of the blue waters of the Bay through the cable slot in the center of the track. In the distance, one can also see the grey island of Alcatraz.

64-65 This remarkable glassed-in atrium is known as the Crocker Gallery. Done up in the latest Eighties architectural style and bearing the name of a major San Francisco bank, it is a three-story-tall shopping center, with sixty stores and two restaurants.

66-67 Along the Embarcadero, just a few hundred yards from San Francisco Bay, street musicians and performers of all sorts — some officially scheduled and others entirely self-employed — perform regularly for the lunchtime crowd.

68 Murals are a popular art form in San Francisco, particularly in the largely Latino Mission District. These paintings depict a wide array of themes, taking their subjects from everyday life, and from the hopes and dreams of the artists. In particular, in the area from Mission Street to York Street, and from Fourteenth Avenue to Army Street, the walls are entirely covered with colorful murals, in which one often sees references to the troubled relationships between the various ethnic groups — Mexicans, Chileans, Cubans, but also Italians, Irish, and Russians — who live in these neighborhoods.

69 This building, completely transformed by the murals that cover it, stands at the intersection of Broadway and Columbus Avenue, in a neighborhood featuring many jazz clubs, founded in the Fifties and Sixties, when the Beat Generation haunted this city. The mural takes its inspiration from the world of music: it features some of the most famous jazz musicians of the century, such as Glenn Miller, Charles Mingus, Lennie Tristano.

70-71 Caffè Trieste, founded in 1956, stands at the corner of Grant and Vallejo. With its water-spotted photos and funky espresso bar, the place has changed little since the days when bearded bards discussed cool jazz and Eisenhower politics.

71 top Caffè Roma is yet another espresso and cappuccino bar in San Francisco's North Beach, the area once haunted by beatniks and fishermen, and now a high rent district of coffee connoisseurs.

71 bottom Caffè Puccini graces the streets of a city that has always had a lot of Italian spirit.

72-73 The Moscone Convention Center, completed in 1981, cost more than one hundred and twenty million dollars. Aside from forty rooms for lectures and conventions, it also boasts an enormous ballroom, which can hold thirty thousand people.

SAN FRANCISCO

74-75 Fisherman's Wharf, once populated by real fishermen, at first Chinese, then Genoans, then Sicilians, has nowadays become a tourist attraction. Here, everything is fun and spectacular: street artists, mimes, and jugglers attract huge crowds, as do the rides and the souvenir shops.

75 top In the picture one can see the famous sign atop the old Ghirardelli Building, and in the background is the clocktower: the complex was built by the Pioneer Woolen Mill and D. Ghirardelli Company, over a period ranging from 1859 to 1915.

75 center Pier 39, which stands at the end of Stockton Street, is a vast complex of stores, restaurants, fishing piers, and craftsmen's workshops, built entirely in wood to resemble a Cape Cod fishing village.

75 bottom Frequented essentially by tourists, Fisherman's Wharf allows one to enjoy unexpected street shows.

SAN FRANCISCO

76-77 San Francisco's Chinatown developed with the Gold Rush, which drew multitudes of fortune-seekers from all over the world; close to twenty thousand Chinese had come to San Francisco to settle by 1852. Tens of thousands more came to work on the western half of the Transcontinental Railroad, which joined the coasts when the last,

"Golden" spike was driven in Provo, Utah. Here we see Chinatown as it is today: rows of restaurants and theaters with odd signs. Here everything has a Chinese theme, and the architecture is exaggerated, and at times over the top: gimmicky telephone booths, lamp posts, and pagoda roofs. Even the Chinatown gate presents the inevitable dragons and typical symbolic motifs of the Chinese decorative architecture.

78-79 The vanguard of the
Saint Patrick's Day Parade
moves up Market Street, in a
tribute to the Irish community
of San Francisco, and to the
patron saint of their
homeland. The Irish are a
powerful presence here.
In these pictures, the statue of
the saint is carried in
procession, and one can see a
flower-bedecked float with the
colors of the Irish flag.

80-81 Nearly half of the people who live in the Mission District are of Latino descent, though by no means are all of them Catholics. Much of the Spanish-speaking immigrants arrive from the Philippines in the Pacific Ocean. This is a vibrant home to the city's Mexican, Colombian, Guatemalan, Nicaraguan, and Salvadoran population. It is a neighborhood where brilliant murals compete with graffiti-crowded walls, and brightly colored festivals recall the atmosphere and traditions of the native lands.

82-83 The Japanese Tea Garden, near the De Young Museum, in Golden Gate Park, is one of the most restful places in San Francisco. In this lovely little park, created in 1894, one can marvel at the admirably disciplined shrubbery, the handsome pagoda structures and splendid high-arch bridges, the rock gardens and the carved stone lanterns. One can stroll past carp-stocked ponds and through hand-wrought gateways.

84-85 San Franciscans enjoy the splendid sunshine, verdant lawn, and excellent view of Mission Dolores Park, a rectangle of rolling hills dotted with magnolia and pepper trees.

SAN FRANCISCO

86-87 The contrast between old and new in San Francisco is highlighted in this photograph. The lovely old structures of the Victorian houses of Alamo Square, built between 1894 and 1895 by Matthew Kavenaugh in the so-called Queen Anne style, seem to clash somewhat with the clean sharp lines of the skyscrapers in the distance.

87 top San Franciscans love their Victorian houses, because they represent a tangible link with the past and with the city's history.

87 right The Painted Ladies were inspired by four principal architectural styles: the Queen Anne style, which was prevalent in England in the second half of the nineteenth century, the Italianate, which referred to the style of the Italian Renaissance, Georgian, which was the dominant style in England between 1702 and 1830, and the Stick style, created by the flair of the English architect, Sir Charles Locke Eastlake.

88-89 These old Victorian houses in Alamo Square are typical of San Francisco, though many of the wood frame houses burned in the blaze that followed the 1906 earthquake. Alamo Square features a continuum of residential design by distinguished architects, spanning the period from the 1870s to the 1920s.

FOG AND THE GOLDEN GATE

Just west of Sausalito, however, is a more permanent connection across the mouth of the bay: the Golden Gate Bridge. The bridge juts southward, separating bay from ocean, thrusting out of the shoulders of the Marin Hills; over these golden sugarloaf shapes pour dense, ambitious fogs rolling down through the pass into the bay. The Golden Gate Bridge was built in the Thirties, certainly one of the great engineering projects of the era. It is a spectacular, twin-pier, suspension bridge, painted ferrous orange and styled in classic deco lines. People intuitively understand that this is a mythic land's-end of remarkable proportions, signifying too much to a troubled few: in fact, the Golden Gate Bridge is a great favorite for suicides, and nearly a

thousand have ended it all, virtually every one of them dropping off the bay side of the bridge, the last sight in their mortal gaze the lovely city on the hill before them. The waters into which these lost souls drop are rough, windswept, and treacherously choppy. So many white crests ripple the turbulent waters that they are known as the Potato Patch; it is a frightening experience to bob through them rapidly in a small sailboat, and Jack London describes even a sizable vessel in dire troubles just off the Golden Gate strait. The bridge's central span is mighty and rises high above the choppy waters below; few captains would think even once about clearance. The nuclear-powered aircraft carrier, Enterprise, however, ventured under the bridge only at low tide; even then, the radar high atop the huge ship's superstructure, had to be tilted on a giant hinge and swayed down, lest it be clipped off neatly as it swept under the latticed orange metal. In absolute, however, the two finest views of the Golden Gate Bridge are from the headlands of Land's End, at the peninsula's northwest tip; and on the corresponding location north of the bridge, Vista Point.

90 The Golden Gate Bridge stands majestically across the landscape, making San Francisco Bay into one of the most remarkable sights in the world. In this photograph, the ocean waves break on the rocks and a slight fog veils everything in a mysterious embrace.

91 The Golden Gate Bridge is certainly one of the best known symbols of San Francisco. Work on its construction, directed by the engineer Joseph Baermann Strauss, began on 5 February 1933; and on 17 May 1937, the bridge was inaugurated, and then opened to traffic on the next day.

SAN FRANCISCO

92-93 The engineer Joseph Strauss had to overcome problems of every sort, defying universal skepticism and the harsh criticism of those who believed that the bridge could never be built. The overall length of the bridge is 8,981 feet, with a single 4,200-foot span; it weighs 123 million pounds, and had a total cost of 35 million dollars. The towers rise to a height of seven hundred and forty-five feet; the main cables are about a yard in diameter.

To the west lies Seal Rock and the Cliff House; to the north is a view inland to the bridge, sidelit by the sunlight of sunset, glowing orange amidst the gray of the fog and the vast grey-green platform of the Pacific main; here, in the failing light of afternoon, one can see the great ships as they come yawing and rolling into the roadstead of the bay, under the Golden Gate. As they sweep up the face of the bay, those ships will pass two islands, one to port, the second to starboard: the first is Angel Island, a lovely, unspoiled, car-free playground for hikers, picknickers, and anchoring sailboaters. The second is equally car-free, but is a tourist attraction for grimmer, even morbid reasons: Alcatraz. Alcatraz was for years America's foremost high-security prison, for incorrigibiles: the Rock. Certainly, it was a refined torture; those few who caught a glimpse of the mainland saw the most beautiful city in America, one of the most beautiful cities on Earth; a few miles away, but as unattainable as yesterday. As Alcatraz was being decommissioned, the only three prisoners to escape set off on their desperate venture: they climbed through the ceilings of their cells, onto a gallery that was no longer guarded due to cutbacks in staff. From here, they scratched their way to the roof, once swept by a searchlight and guard tower, but now unmanned. Over the side and into the water, on a hand-made inflatable raft. One was found nearly dead, washed up on the shore; one was picked up by a launch; the third was never seen again, swept away in the night — the local mythology has it that he escaped successfully. Although it was frowned upon by the authorities, and happened infrequently, during World War II, when San Francisco was home base to many air squadrons, some of the more daring flyboys would pilot their P-38s and Mustangs under the bridge. The real daredevils went through at high tide, doing wing rolls over the choppy white waters of the Potato Patch. The bridge was built across a stretch of water bedeviled by fog; the

following description captures it nicely: "The fog comes in — an army of ghostly sky-riders, a changing trampling herd of formless wraiths." That and the powerful Pacific currents provided twin challenges to Joseph Baermann Strauss, mastermind and builder of the Golden Gate Bridge, who in college had already designed a bridge across the Bering Strait. The Golden Gate was opened on 27 May 1937, a structure 8,981 feet in length, with a single 4,200-foot span, weighing 123 million pounds, at a total cost of 35 million dollars. The south tower was the most challenging to be build, standing 1,125 feet offshore. In order to build it, a fender was built in the roaring rushing ocean depths. This astonishing piece of engineering stands amidst a vast sea of tumultuous elements. As the famous writer Herold Gilliam described it, "A long finger of fog slips in through the Golden Gate just over the water, sometimes beneath the deck of the bridge..." Another guide book suggested going to Vista Point, just north of the bridge, about noon on a summer day: "There you command a view comparable to that from the lookout point at the brink of Niagara. Standing in the sun, you face a river of fog that may be a mile wide and hundreds of feet deep." And lastly, let us close with a description of the bridge at the end of day: "All day a moving cloud canopy has hung over the gray bay, occasionally trailing long banners of rain which stippled the waters and gently sprinkled the shores. Now, at day's end, comes a violent transformation. The sun had descended beneath the western edge of the canopy and floods the bay and its shores with light. "The bridge at the narrows is black against the sun, and in the sky beyond it are long glowing bars of cloud strata, radiating feathery banners of flame. The water surface, the misty air, and the clouds are suffused with golden opalescence. Again, as in early spring, the cities climbing the East Bay hills are ablaze with the reflected light of the western sky." San Francisco opens her Golden Gates to the world.

94-95 The water is rough, and so are the winds, and so sports fans of all sorts congregate in the lee of the Golden Gate Bridge. The sailboat enthusiasts are far more common than are the windsurfers, and they in turn more common than surfers, and yet we offer a photograph of one or two of each enjoying the view and daring the elements in some of the roughest waters around.

96-97 When admiring the Golden Gate Bridge from up close, one can fully appreciate the majestic dimensions and the simplicity of the design. It may help to grasp the engineering involved to note that the construction of the bridge required twenty thousand tons of steel and eighty miles of cable.

98-99 The Golden Gate Bridge may be a great many things to a great many people, but to many San Franciscans it is an excellent place to exercise, whether that means long-distance running or equally long-distance bicycling, to Stinson Beach and points even further north.

SAN FRANCISCO

100-101 At the entrance to San Francisco Bay, the wind can be fierce and terrific, subjecting the structure of the Golden Gate Bridge to tremendous strains: suffice it to think that when the wind blows at a hundred miles an hour, the roadbed of the

bridge swings through an arc of nearly twenty feet. And, depending on temperature and traffic intensity, the roadbed may be raised or lowered as much as sixteen feet.

102-103 In order to maintain the bridge's splendid orange hue, it takes ten thousand gallons of paint every year.

104-105 The Golden Gate Bridge holds a number of unusual records. On the one hand, it has the lowest number of deaths among the workers who built it for any bridge its size; on the other, it boasts the lugubrious record of having the highest number of suicides.

106-107 The Golden Gate Bridge is seen here awash in a major bank of fog. One author described this scene in the following words: "The fog comes in — an army of ghostly sky-riders, a changing trampling herd of formless wraiths."

CITY LIGHTS

Thus is the stage set: with islands, ocean currents, broad headlands, and mighty hills; across that stage sweeps the wind and creeps San Francisco's oldest, largest, quietest, and most mysterious inhabitant: the fog. San Francisco's fog — with its two allies, the Pacific winds and the city's hills — make this a place apart; even when the sun shines brightly, high-flying clouds sail through the rays, louring to foreshadow lurking fog. The fog has such an intense physical presence that more than one new inhabitant of the city has been disconcerted. One shop clerk, astonished at the sight of a cloud of billowing white smoke, ran out to the street to check. Sure enough, she thought, it

was pouring down the street so fast and in such volume that it could only be a building on fire. She ran back into the store, alerting her boss to the sudden emergency, who came rushing out into the street to see. He turned to her with a smirk, and said, that's no fire, just fog. The warmer the season, the more fog there is, and the more fog there is, the colder it gets: Mark Twain, as San Franciscans never tired of relating, once said, "The coldest winter I ever spent was a summer in San Francisco." The light here is more nuanced and richly textured than elsewhere; mottled, striated, pitted, tattersalled by the scudding mist and cloud. This light is meltingly lovely, gray and red, mixed with foreboding and nostalgia. An aerial navigator, for example, appreciates, as few others may, the hushed, intimate contact between fog, light, and the city. Guy Murchie, a veteran navigator, wrote the following about San Francisco and its fog. "Streaky, sooty fogs from the sky can be as beautiful as the purest marble. "They are slow-moving seas or fast-flowing glaciers - rivers of vapor that reveal the wimpling and snurling of air as plainly as brooks show the rippling of water - by day their

108 Lights appear across the water from Alcatraz, the former Federal high-security prison, answered by lights from the fishing and pleasure boats docked at Fisherman's Wharf.

109 Lights begin to turn on in the homes and in the nightspots along San Francisco's Columbus Avenue, and to blink off in the windows of the office buildings in the city's Financial District.

whorls gray and brown, sometimes with interfolds of yellow, lavender, or red - by night the lights of cities pulsing dimly through this glowing flesh of the weary brow of earth. "Once I saw San Francisco blinking up at me through such a mottled shroud that it seemed the hidden heart of a strange planet. Car and street lights of every color flashed on and off in weird contrapuntal rhythm through holes and thin spots of the moving fog. "If one had descended upon Saturn or Pluto to behold a similar sight I can imagine the awe it would inspire." And if the light of San Francisco is lovely in the fog, so is the darkness. From high atop Twin Peaks, the whole city stretches out, all the winding streets turned into coiled necklaces of street lights and the buildings spangled with glittering windows. If the fog is running, it clusters close, narrowing your gaze; if it lifts, or the night is entirely clear, then one can see the complete panorama: the city jutting north out into a vast tableland of water, the Pacific to the west and the bay to the east; the elegant airy arches of the bridges outlined in chains of light and streamers of bright automobiles; the apparent lava-flow of luminosity of the East Bay, oozing from the high hills down to the flat waterfront. Above Coit Tower are piercing white shafts of searchlight, through which the patches and tattered sheets of fog move briskly.

In short, San Francisco is gorgeous and alluring by night. It has been said that San Francisco is like an achingly beautiful yet appallingly dumb girlfriend (or boyfriend). This may be because of its fascinatingly monotonous repetition of the same exquisite themes: fog, poignant splendor, steep hills, ocean views, architecture redolent of the Twenties. If so, there is only one way to treat a dumb but beautiful girlfriend (or boyfriend) by night.

And that is to get out the old motorcycle (for this city, a small pony-like bike is recommended, say, a Honda 400 Sport or some such. Saddle up, and set out on the best way

110 The Clocktower of Ghirardelli Square was built in 1915 on the model of the tower of the Château de Blois, in France. The factory was converted in the Fifties, into what was to become a model for many other such conversions across the country.

111 top At the foot of the hills, lights glitter on Fisherman's Wharf; high in the background are Telegraph Hill with Coit Tower, and further off, the Transamerica Pyramid.

111 bottom Dusk falls and lights flicker on at Ghirardelli Square, the great shopping avenue for souvenirs and memorabilia only a few yards from Fisherman's Wharf. This is the perfect departure point for a cable-car ride through darkness and fog over Russian and Nob hills.

112 Not even nightfall slows life in the streets of the center of San Francisco. The lights of the buildings, and the streetlights, transform the usual appearance of San Francisco, emphasizing its exuberant and refined beauty.

113 In Union Square, the neon sign of Macy's department glitters at night, one of the great shopping centers of the city.

114-115 The lavish lighting of an amusement park makes this merry-go-round on Pier 39 into something that, as one writer put it, makes Disneyland look real. In the background are Telegraph Hill, with Coit Tower, and further off, the Transamerica Pyramid.

116-117 This is San Francisco's Strip of nightclubs and stripjoints, where Columbus Avenue intersects with Broadway.

to see San Francisco at her most hauntingly beautiful and romantically adventurous. The motorcycle in San Francisco is a different mechanical contrivance — the tendency is not to ride it on a straight-line course, but ducking bobbing and weaving, testing the grip of the pavement and the attack of the grade, especially in descent, the best position for viewing anyway. With a motorcycle, the views that may be attractive on foot become dramatic — to put it in cinematic terms, the camera is suddenly mounted on a gurney, and unimaginable degrees of liberty are instantly obtained. And one is propelled upward, round panoramic curves, along alleys that suddenly open out to vast hilltop views, and up dirt paths and into parks of wind-tossed bushes and trees. From a motorcycle San Francisco by night becomes a rapid succession of moonlit and starlit vistas, streetlights drumming by, kinetoscopic successions of lighted windows, and sage and pine in the dewy coolth of the Presidio or Fort Point, beneath the bridge. The best and most exciting of all the motorcycle views of San Francisco however is this: ride down on Route 101 from the north, say from Bodega Bay (where Hitchcock filmed "The Birds") or Jenner, on the Russian River. Take a big Harley — no Honda 400s for this ride. Let her rip; the idea is to touch 100 mph at some point during the ride — as wrong and dangerous and inadvisable as this may be. And then settle down for the last leg of the trip, when you burst out of the smoky and pine-scented Marin darkness onto the rust-orange of the Golden Gate bridge and spotlights and vast Pacific with its airy tang and — off to the left — the city for which you were willing to risk suicide on a big heavy dangerous bike, glittering and toppling and fog-laden in the moonlight. And for all you know, you did have a crash and this is your immortal soul unburdened by bodily flesh crossing the Golden Gate; after all, as Oscar Wilde points out earlier in the book: San Francisco has all the attractions of the next world.

SAN FRANCISCO

118-119 Looking down Mission Street in the gathering dusk, one can see Twin Peaks off to the right; here night falls on one of the most suburban and yet hilliest areas of San Francisco.

119 top In the distance stands the Ferry Building, at the Embarcadero at Market Street. This is the most readily identifiable building in the city, thanks to the tower. Completed in 1903, the tower stands two hundred and thirty-five feet high, and is modeled after the Giralda of the Cathedral of Seville, Spain.

119 bottom Lighted cars and cable cars climb up Powell Street past the chic area of Union Square. Although it is nighttime this far down the hill, full daylight can be seen to the west, above the hill.

120 Culture is as much of a presence in the city as the fog, and ranges from opera to kabuki to drag theater to some of the most rocking music of the past thirty years: from the Grateful Dead, the Jefferson Airplane and Janis Joplin to Tuxedo Moon, Romeo Void, and the Dead Kennedys. Rock venues hop, in particular; this is a typical scene in a local rock club.

121 San Francisco is home to numerous different ethnic groups, which keep customs and traditions intact. Cuisine, too, forms part of a people's cultural heritage, and all over the city, one finds restaurants serving dishes from all over the world. Here, one can see the interior of Tommy's, a popular local Mexican restaurant.

122-123 Bright red, brilliant green, canary yellow: these are the colors that predominate in the electric signs that light up Chinatown by night. These distintive and characteristic neon signs and colored bulbs reproduce Chinese characters. In this neighborhood, the street life goes on till late at night, while restaurants and food shops remain open until the wee hours.

124-125 San Francisco City Hall, which looms huge against a sky striped by the fading light of the sun, was built between 1913 and 1915. Designed by the architect Arthur Brown, and clearly taking inspiration from the classic French style, this monumental building rises on a rectangular base measuring three hundred and ninety-four feet by two hundred and ninety-five, topped by a mighty cupola.

128 The reddish light of sunset enhances and silhouettes the futuristic shape of the Transamerica Pyramid.

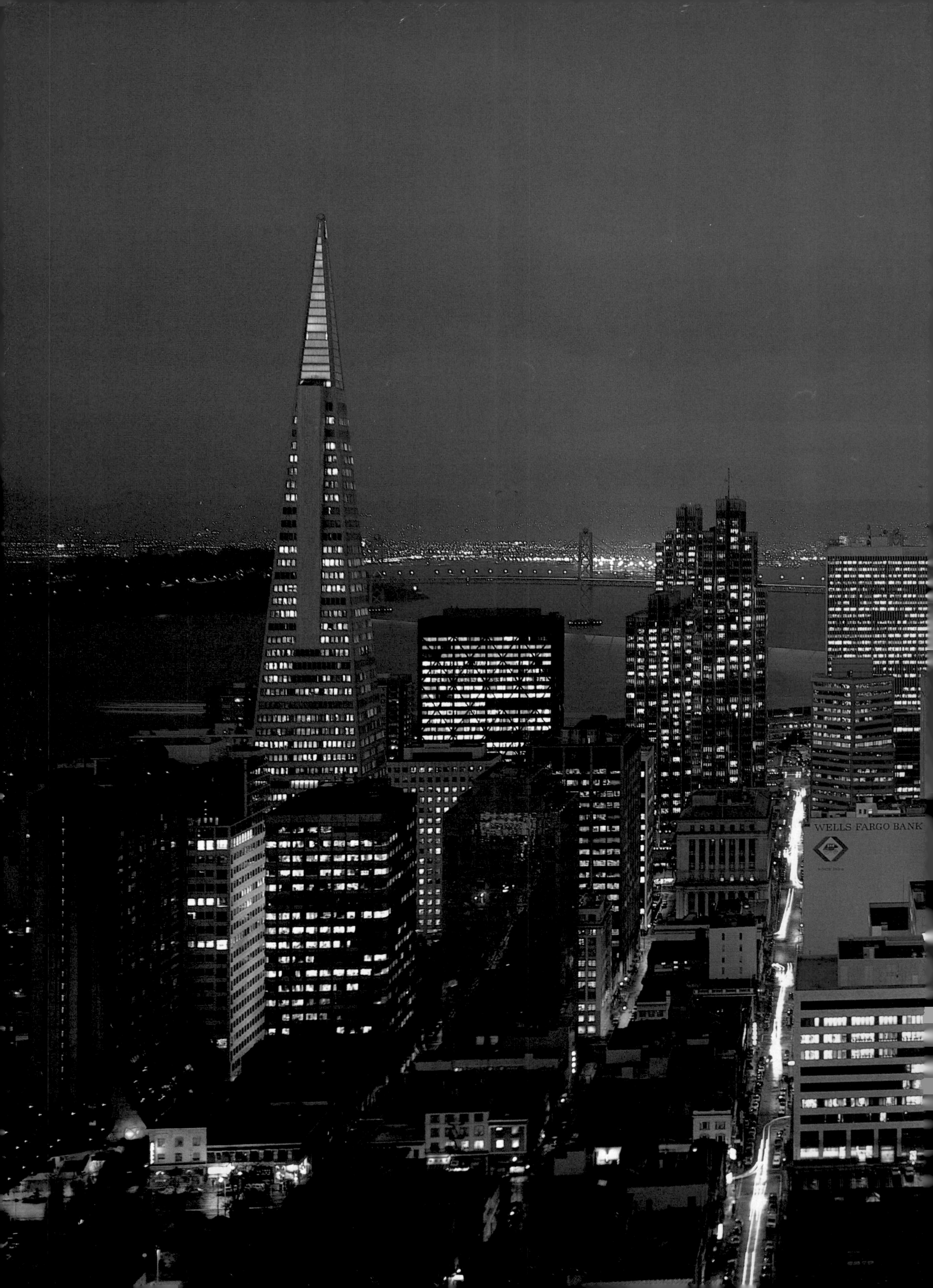
WELLS FARGO BANK

SAN FRANCISCO

PHOTO CREDITS